Anniversary Wings

Poems

Anniversary Wings

Poems
Centric
and
Eccentric

William N. Gates

SUNSTONE
PRESS

SANTA FE

Sunstone books may be purchased for educational, business, or sales promotional use. For information please write: Special Markets Department, Sunstone Press, P.O. Box 2321, Santa Fe, New Mexico 87504-2321.

Book and cover design › Vicki Ahl
Body typeface › Adobe Jenson Pro
Printed on acid-free paper
∞
eBook 978-1-61139-471-9

Library of Congress Cataloging-in-Publication Data

Names: Gates, William N., 1930- author.
Title: Anniversary wings : poems centric and eccentric / by William N. Gates.
Description: Santa Fe : Sunstone Press, [2016]
Identifiers: LCCN 2016013002 (print) | LCCN 2016020093 (ebook) | ISBN 9781632931320 (softcover : alk. paper) | ISBN 9781611394719
Classification: LCC PS3607.A7888 A6 2016 (print) | LCC PS3607.A7888 (ebook) | DDC 811/.6--dc23
LC record available at https://lccn.loc.gov/2016013002

SUNSTONE PRESS IS COMMITTED TO MINIMIZING OUR ENVIRONMENTAL IMPACT ON THE PLANET. THE PAPER USED IN THIS BOOK IS FROM RESPONSIBLY MANAGED FORESTS. OUR PRINTER HAS RECEIVED CHAIN OF CUSTODY (COC) CERTIFICATION FROM: THE FOREST STEWARDSHIP COUNCIL™ (FSC®), PROGRAMME FOR THE ENDORSEMENT OF FOREST CERTIFICATION™ (PEFC™), AND THE SUSTAINABLE FORESTRY INITIATIVE® (SFI®). THE FSC® COUNCIL IS A NON-PROFIT ORGANIZATION, PROMOTING THE ENVIRONMENTALLY APPROPRIATE, SOCIALLY BENEFICIAL AND ECONOMICALLY VIABLE MANAGEMENT OF THE WORLD'S FORESTS. FSC® CERTIFICATION IS RECOGNIZED INTERNATIONALLY AS A RIGOROUS ENVIRONMENTAL AND SOCIAL STANDARD FOR RESPONSIBLE FOREST MANAGEMENT.

WWW.SUNSTONEPRESS.COM
SUNSTONE PRESS / POST OFFICE BOX 2321 / SANTA FE, NM 87504-2321 /USA
(505) 988-4418 / ORDERS ONLY (800) 243-5644 / FAX (505) 988-1025

Contents

Anniversary Wings / 43

Convergence / 69

Grandmother Summer

Grandmother Summer

Gnats and flies whirl in a craze,
Pods of milkweed store their swarms
Of aerial seeds through sultry days.

Black and shining sidelights eye
A screen door that hangs agog
At shocks of children tearing by.

Phoebe's oboe cries wee
In concert of children, crow, cow,
Swell and fall of oceanic tree.

Upstairs the sovereign of the children
Writes in the breeze of electric fan,
Ice cube placed in her knot of bun

To run a trickle down her nape.
Face in a round and royal smile
She drives her pen across the paper,

Fills a teeming letter pouch,
Others' enveloped with hers
For keeping everyone in touch.

No way to mend the broken parents,

Just hug the young, and write and save
Crops of answers, nutriments

Packed in boxes, time seed
To conjure stalks and blooms of people,
These among her goods to deed.

Jay

A bird called
And cued a day
I'd left behind:

When
I scouted
Down a myrtled
Bank through budding
Trees to a crocodile snag
And venomous mud-torpid river
Dozing past backyards of far-shore
Houses in grandmother's town and life:

A child I held
The 2 cheers
Of jay in mind.

Disappearance

I

Home from school one winter's day
The child found his mother gone
With no good-bye, no word to him.

Father, maid, everybody
Knew but kept him in the dark
Because she couldn't bear to face him.

Twice more they met before the War.
First time, he watched her slide away
By train, then on across the ocean.

Tears couldn't hold her there,
Tears wouldn't bring her back,
Tears only made her cross.

Next time his father (and his bride)
Took him on an ocean liner
To see his mother (and her groom).

She took him to the London Zoo
And to the movies, bought him toys,
A Spitfire and a panda puppet.

He knew there'd be an end to this.

A gliding door would close her off,
Her good-bye face seen in a blur.

> "My Bonnie lies over the ocean,
> My Bonnie lies over the sea,
> O bring back my Bonnie to me –"

A teasing song. Came a letter
From her, overhead she saw
A Messerschmitt pursue a Spitfire.
He dreamed she was killed in the Blitz.

II

Now the War was past, she paid
A visit to her old home town,
Not with face or form he knew,
An apparition, short and thick.

"Get me a drink," she barked at her spouse
Back from years in the British Army.
With other wives she'd waited years,
Lonely under deadly skies.

Eighteen he sailed abroad to her.
Called her "Ma," which seemed to fit.
To ease the guilt she may have felt
He said he didn't need a mother.

She liked elaborate dirty jokes.
He could play her game of jokes,
They laughed together, drank together.
On night her friend pulled him aside,

Said, "She adores you," kissed his lips
To print it on him. Ma was drunk,
They all were drunk, he let it pass,
Confused by words and a smear of lipstick.

At twenty-one she cornered him,
"You're sulking, you're not giving."
He turned to staring out the window,
Another dismal day in England.

More and more he kept to himself
As he outgrew the two of them.
Now their lives seemed in reverse
As he was the one to pull away.

One last time he went to see her,
Shriveled, starved by Crohn's disease.
One more year she clung and then
She definitely disappeared.

She'd kept a portrait of him at seven,
Placed it right above her hearth.
He looked at her with trusting eyes,

Face to face, no tears or doubts.
She knew in leaving him she'd lost him.

III

Vanishing reverberates:
Jealousy's an outward fury
Puts a mask on fear of loss
Of someone precious and of self.

In his old age he dreams a nosy
Apparition corners him:
"Don't you feel upset about
The boyfriend?" Who? Whose boyfriend?

"He's from the South," she warns.
He's too old to be upset
But not so old as not to feel
A twinge, an echo of alarm

Harking back and back to a day
In Thirty-Eight, when a hunk of him
Sheered off and left a wisp of self,
And trust and tears well hidden.

Farm Volunteers, 1945

We harvesters of summer '45,
We stooped in spinach or crawled along the corn
And throb of bombers burning paper cities
Was less to us than mutter of inside boogie,
Less to us than muggy haze and sweatbees
Coaxing us to kill the time till noon
And fade toward the shade where the water was parked.

Evenings in the camp we crowded round
Where Pete was playing "Down the Road Apiece"
(Better than chicken fried in bacon grease)
And Freddy danced with Ruthy, one and all
Danced and swayed and got a goodnight kiss
But me (Oh beat me Daddy, eight to the bar)
I studied how to play that boogie woogie.

Mornings Grant chose one of us to say
A grace, while Betty and Bonny made our lunches.
And when we threw a banquet near the end
They mopped up like tired beaten parents.
Their Christian voices mumbled off to silence.
And when the bomb was dropped on Nagasaki
Fire reached around the world to touch us:

A shout went up, horns and whistles blared,
Everybody was running out and hugging,
Quick I squeezed the prettiest girl and ran.
Seeds of understanding flashed away,
Parched by war, ashed by victory.
And now here came a brand new junior army,
Learning how to smoke and kiss goodnight.

In Memoriam
August 2005

Cease-Fire, 1973

Falls a lull,
A booby-trapped hush
A sneeze would snap,
A nod to run and fetch the gauze
Of hours or years to stanch
The wounds and hide the stain.

Born in the 1930s
Let us share the bones we keep.
"Peace" is a hedger's oath,
"Pray for Peace," words hollow
As our mocking skulls.
So long as men are men
Children will die.

As children we survived the "Good" war
Yet a fine gut thread binds us
To the dead slaughtered young as we,
Trapped by nationality.

They gapped our voice, they left
A silence and a gnaw. They took our faith,
They left us hanging back.
They are our lost, our missing.
A shift in oceanic luck
And we were they, naked,
Manforsaken.

Terror
arrow

sorrow

harrow
her

Khmer
child
chilled
girl

unfurls
hands

stance

dancer

tower

Messages from Kitty

Dear Anne, I took you in, but then
  I couldn't keep you secret. You've
  Been found, they've made a play of you
  And now you're starring on the screen.
  She's nothing like the real you.

Dear Anne, "I still believe that people
  Are good at heart": do you say that
  Now you know how bad they are?
  If still you say so then I can't
  Dismiss the possibility.

Dear Anne, you've been proclaimed a "genius,"
  Your diary a "masterpiece."
  You also wrote: "There is in people
  An urge to destroy, to kill, to murder."
  I miss the real you. Just give
  A sign; you I will believe.

Tidings

The slow word,

Horse-drawn, boat-borne

Word went riding, canoeing,

Word grew gray and weedy wandering;

When it came they'd given up waiting,

Moved away, grown used to making do;

When word arrived they turned it out

To graze with other ancient tidings.

Pine Soldier Fence

The tall, the short, the cracked and gaunt,
The tattered slabs of bark in rank,
Nailed and dressed and drawn up straight,
Wobbled by wind and razzed by crows,
The hollow square of veterans stands
And guards a plot of carrots and corn.
"Never relent. Never relent."

Nobody told them war was done.
(The only sniper in all that time,
A flicker tapping their coats for a snack.)
And now what good in years of calm
To try to return, collect their lives,
Reclaim the loves who kissed them off.
Best to ignore the signs of peace,
The whisper of crops behind their backs.
"Never relent. Our good is spent."

Guidelines

To proceed: first we string
Our batterboards from nail to nail
And stretch and tune our plan midair.
Next, to cast this diagram
Of cord upon the ground we pick
A sharp and heavy bullet, name of
Plumbob, tie him to the line.
Bullet Bob he dangles plumb
And where he points we stick a stake;
Slide him farther, let him bob
Another dot and stake it so.
Run a string between, and take
Our can of lime and pinch its lip
And shake the powder down the string-line.
So on, leap-frog, Bob and lime,
Until we have a nice white print
Of house on dirt. Any fool
Can do it, just don't scuff and don't
Rile the wind, wind erases.

To Build a House

Across the dirt they spread the plans,
Pinned them down with a rock and a brick.
The builders puzzled, then began
To string a copy in the air.

The draftsman came to peer and scan;
They gouged a thicker print in earth.
When they double-checked their spans
They found a step they'd overlooked.

The drawings flashed complex demands
And rolled up tight like window-shades.
Began a battle of plans and the hands
That tried to realize their worth.

But the house had a will of its own, command
Of adobe mass and mud and sand;
And how it would bulk upon the land
Had little to do with men or plans.

House Born of Mud

See how the weeds and lizards board
The bleached gun'ls of mortar box beached
On a crackled hill, that one time plowed
Seas of dirt, lugging and cradling
Cargos of mezcla batched by a mud-cook.

Hoe for a spoon, he chopped a batter
Of earth and water, sand and straw,
Drove it and hauled it until it slapped
A luscious mush that wheelbarrows ferried
To scaffolds of bakers building a cake
As big as a house.

           Eager to home,
Its creators came for the salvage or solace
Of newborn rooms. The blank of the future
Was building a shape before their eyes.
The children would make the place their own
By play and fear and window theaters,
Their refuge from school, palace of Christmas,
Wedding chapel.

           But time would come—
What jolt to them then to know
How short their time would be—which in

Its slow exploding and dispersing
(No time for a wedding) they'd accept
As right, when they would leave their house,
Their harbor, and go their separate ways.

Born of mud and desire for beauty
The house would stand a home or a stage
For others, maybe for generations.
All of it hatched from that wreck of a cradle
Beached on the side of a burnt-out hill.

Erased Places

The road we strolled would disappear.
The grove we camped in, razed and blacktopped.
Our ship to Europe sold for scrap,
The patio where we hatched our future
Roofed and boxed in little rooms.

Rubbed-out places bare to me
The failure of youth, the fortune lost.
Try as we would with all our will
Time and hope and adoration
Poured away. Only endures
Desire's huge and loaded tree,
Not rooted any place
But making up for loss.

After All There Was This

One morning years ago
I saw our bedroom curtains
Lifting in a breeze,
Tall cloudy skirts with weights
That fell from pleats into grays,
Whites and then peach lights
Of the rising sun and thin
Bars of window shadow.

She'd gone back to sleep
And I lay watching this
Countervailing play.
What she kept from me
We agreed she could not give,
And what I kept from her
I wouldn't give or say.
The struggle thinned us down
To what we had, and that
We assured ourselves was enough
To hold us, let alone
Our children or the house
We'd made.

                    And after all
The worn-out night fell away,
Gave way to breezy cool
And swaying dawn of cloth,
Pale peach window lights
Playing in the white.

Exit She

She stole away, leaving a note.
The end, so many times imagined;
Or would they patch it up.
He packed a bag, slammed the door
On the telephone and drove away.

Each night he stopped another place,
Each night unsnapped his case
And released a folded spook
That kept him waking, writhing.

Sleep-lack drove him back.
From far he saw the heat, the haze.
Traffic thickened as he neared,
As he raced to smash the thing he feared.

Combat

A gun is rapping for attention
Somewhere beyond the jut of building,
Or is it a jackhammer at the corner
Chopping out another ramp
For the wheelchair army, or someone
At the door, or a heavy caliber
Typewriter overhead—
Someone's out to kill the quiet,
Blow me out of sleep and dream.
It's only Philadelphia,
June of Nineteen Seventy-Nine,
And she is gone and I'm alone.

Toll
token
taken
dole
spokesman

corridor
roaring
door
rolling
holler

cellar
yell
hole
cramming
screaming
hubbub
sub
-terranean
rocket
racket
rocking
dolts
jolted

rout

sub
-urb
bound
binned
bums
glum

grumble
stumble
out

Razing

No castle, church or temple shell,
No ancient building woebegone
Would kin this shocked hulk of brick
With its knocked-out front, its naked side
A palette of cream, pink, blue
Divided by umber scars of wall,
Floor and stair
                      which they raze
And in its place another face
Compose of look-alike brick
That will not crumble, and so raise
The lasting ruins of the future.

Fell Hand

"—by Time's fell hand defaced—"

You must be grim, and scrape and pare
And whittle down potatoes if
You want to take out every dent.
The deepest wrinkles disappear
Only if you trim severely,
Convert potato to an egg.

Take this stone, that has a slit
Dug in its perfect silky side
Gives it an obstinate expression,
Sea would have to rasp and grind
For years, rub it down to grit
To delete that stubborn look.

I know someone who bears a look
With eyelids shuttered down at corners,
Still shows a sliver of defiance
That when he's gone will vanish in the bone.

Sea's not satisfied with sand
And strokes it with a fell hand.

Spring, 1979

Where would I decide to be—
Here or there, this state or that—
Choice I could not see.

No wavering, no U-turn
Allowed on the road I drove
Which zoomed over waves, then dove

To tunnel under passing ships,
Then rose again to resume
Its twenty-mile beeline.

I observed fidelity
To this bridge of strict design.
But it came to me the key

Was to sustain my not deciding,
Keep straddling not siding,
Keep scheming to be free.

But everything was changing.
Twenty-three years of us
Were floating out to sea,

The trusty ice of marriage
Was breaking up and drifting,
And I, nowhere to be.

Return

Fog warmed by a button of sun,
Salads of kelp fussed by fleas,
Blotches of tar, trash and crab-chaw,
Drawn in a trance through all of this
Down to a kind of smile spreading
Whiter than mist, a ceaseless *haaa*—

There was a time we worshiped there
We five as at a sacred temple;
The waves gave all divinity,
All the jubilance we could want.
Ritually we came to gaze,
To breathe the sea and revel in it.

We changed, Ocean, went our ways.
We are no more, we disappeared
Outworn as any family, any year.
But I can play a certain trick,
I can still return to you.

Trees and mountains will remind me.
Even in a landlocked mind,
Through the smog, the jangle and junk,
I hear you and I'm back to you,
Tumbling inexhaustible Now.

Fall, 1979

Fire popped blue
Below a round kettle
That rocked a restless burden,

As once I'd cradled crying
Children, swaying, soothing,
Traipsing room to room,
Acquainting them with mirrors
To eye themselves to calm.

I watched the round kettle
Rock itself to stillness
And wondered where I was,
Where was I to settle,
How begin again.

Now

Now in rapid time
Do you recall your small
Self struggling to scale
Mountainous rounds of the clock
When life stalled in stale
Textbooks, hot back seats,
Sickbed nights, and summers
Slack as an empty windsock?

Now runs more to your liking,
Not yet uneasiness,
Grip of monster current
Pulling shores, houses,
People past and gone
Before you can see or say.

Suitor

Choose me, peruse me,
Ease me from the pack.
Let your eyes appraise
My pattern, my device.
My suit and colors please,
Add the points you seek.
You know I'm good for you,
Feel my numbers vibrate,
I tingle in your pinch.
Let other fingers touch,
Then slide me into place.
I complete your hand.

Glissade

What brows, what lashes to enhance
Your laziest glance, so easily
Your eyes seize me, so I can't
Withdraw from them or swerve my gaze
Toward the margin of your cheek.
You've got me in a hazel trance.
I wonder could you slowly dance
Me out of town, past the stare
Of crowds and blare of music store,
Past the clash of shopping carts,
Miasma of the noontime sizzle,
Past a flutter, a car-lot dazzle,
Till we arrive at daisies whisked
By cars that honk and goggle at us,
Which you sidestep deftly, guide
And glide me to a nook you've chosen
In golden rod and Queen Anne's lace
And minimum of quiet trash.

Anniversary Wings

Comice Promise

share rare
pear's pared
cheerful tears sheer
clear fairest fare comely
Comice comfort ( ) nonpareil be-
yond compare peerless poire ex-
traordinaire debonair paragon pot-
able portly paradisiacal pear

Wraith Racing

        racing
                    writhe
    scathe
                        seethe
                            breath
            scatter
    bitter
            crystals
                        glisten
                                    pristine
                                particles
                        sparkling
            curled
                    whirls
                            frore
                    froth

Wilderness Sky

An icy tracer cuts the blue,
Self-erasing east to west,
Skating fast without a sound;
A second blade southwest-northeast
Transects the first.

Below the high dissolving X
White as the snow their feet are marking,
Ears of bobcat, fox and deer
Stare and track the wake of sound,
A kind of distant winter thunder.

Two Windows on a Blizzard

They waver, then they panic.
See them rushing by—
Now they're swirling back,
Mobs of wispy white
Driven by a force,
Herded by a fear.
I hear no shout, no shot.
In silence beyond a glass
It happens, the fall of masses,
Destiny of flakes.

Air seems to struggle
To escape spots' betraying.
It twists and rears and boxes
Like an invisible leopard
To shake the dots that would stick
And show its least shiver.

Sheets

flung

twisting   tossed

complex   gesture

crumpling   wrinkling

intricate

spilled

sprawl

heaps

lifted   floated

clouds   cloth

binding   envelope   taut   tucked

textile   reclined   plain

molded   smooth

polar

dawn

Late Winter City

Mourn
dour
dawn
endure
diurnal
dirge

come
communal
carmine
flier
crier

wheat
wheat
cue cue cue cue
cure
cure
wit wit wit wit

poor
morn
adorn

Seasonal Questions

Grimy along the streets of town,
Scraps of snow, tenacious ice.
Unfazed the cardinal and the crocus
Assure they will bring in the spring.

Question is, who will notice?
Spring will never make the headlines,
Won't console the burdened man,
Distract the agitated woman.

But here, heedless of attention,
An azalea's about to burst.
Can we discern its innate tints,
Hints of blue that hum in the red?

D's for Dickinson

Deer-dash   dandelion-down   diadem
Daring   despair   distant   dissident   decorous
Debonair   death-bride   daughter   dragonfly-darter
Daedal-eliding   delicate   desolate   droll

Downward Path

Path
    acrid-accurate
      wrath
        boundless bound
      downward
        death-drawn
        droll
        dance
          sparks
           charred words
          blacks crackling
          bountiful
          skull
          sportive mortal
          pungent
          pith
           Plath

Another Life, Another World

Keep to that hard trail
And sure enough you'll find
The twisted stump of spruce,
Shorn of bark to show
Its grain, as of a hand
Revolving as it rises
With lines strictly parallel,
Close but never meeting.

Monument of torsion
Or confined warp
Of a fated marriage, each
In a fight to save some sap
Of self, a splinter of love
Or truth, forlornly close,
Intimately near,
Never to come together.

Anniversary Wings

In Taos high country, summer once,
Up Long Canyon Trail I climbed
To a mountain's scruff, all rock and wind
And crooked wood huddling low.
But there magenta paintbrush bloomed
And pointed to another magic,
A shell of tree, a gray relic
Carved like Winged Victory,
Two pinions from a writhing core.
Dry and light it was to lift
And pack it back the long way down.

You named it not for years of wedlock
But for escape, for our rebirth.
Flower and wood reminded us
That we had overcome the past,
That warped and frozen lives could mix
And melt and come up potent petals.

Late Winter Dreams

Somewhere between the gritty earth
And the sinuous sweeps of cirrus
We heard the warble of geese
Calling to each other
In their wavery progress north.
And when they sometimes circled
Sun would catch them in a sparkle.
Delight you took in them
Would form your favorite moment,
Your amulet to take to sleep.

You dreamed a crowd of strangers
Barged into your house,
You could not drive them out.
A train of implication
Coupled former torments
And dragged you to a standstill.
You felt so small and weak.
But such is your resilience
Wild geese and I could comfort you.

Three silver horns played
"Moonglow," I saw you and
You came to dance with me,
And I would dance with you

But I was torn awake.
Did I desert my joy,
Or did noise destroy—

A coyote shriek, a crack
In a joist—you and music
Were there asleep beside me.
If you lose me in your dreams
I'm ever wrapped around you.

Santa Fe Nights

Coyotes are echoing bygone fiestas.
Piñon firewood, piñon coals
Smolder, refine an incense of smoke.
Dry leaves of cottonwood are hustling.
Train horn mourns. An all-night hauler
Labors up the northbound hill.
Half-moon peers blurred by cloud.
But the dark is luminous enough
To see the rounded cub-like foothills
Climbing toward their mother mountains.
Years of nights resound in one.
Years of writing can radiate
Within a word, a kindling word.
In a dream our long-dead friend
Lives again. New friends are born.
Years of nights resound in one.

Canyon in May

Various
verging
vernal
verd

verdure
uprising
surprising
screening

solemn
columnar
conifers
greening

bird
voyager
tanager
lured

May Melt

Dissolve

  dehisce

   descent

   intent

   extreme

  streaming

strong

        stone

 tone

          timbale

timbre

       foam

  drome

   thronging

  sonance

  utter

  waters

   straying

  staying

  wove

  wave

  was

  were

  are

  is

Screen Time

Time to trim a summer door,
Saw it short, plane the edge,
Walk it to its frame.
A shingle shims it plumb
To mate the hinges, lock the slam.
Slack old screens attend:

A new swinger's tuned to hum,
To sieve the nervous wind.
Children rasp the mesh,
Press noses crosshatch
And coax the cat to climb
By claws picking tiny rungs.

Hypnotic

Recur
purr

bestir
fur

recur-
l

rever-
b
her

per-
fect
mur-
mur

Bandelier Canyon

Eye to eye you and I
Dusk of the day we roved
A pink and green ravine
Up a cold vein of stream
Where turquoise turrets
Rose to ocher parapets
To carmine gargoyles
You tracked my hips
Twisting with the trail
I heard you simmering
Not too late I found you
Grabbed you not too late
In good sweet time we were
All in good time we lay
Eye to ay.

Tune
2-tine
fork
hark

A
ah
hey
olé
oyé

aye
yea
ja
yeah
you
coo

moo
moon
mood
com-
modious

moan

mono

-toning

tuning

blue

croon

Some Early Morning

In a dozy float of mind
Came a hint of chord
And tint of ocher autumn,
Plonk and pungent donk
Of banjo backed by bass;
Then a cross-town wake-up
Railing, grumbling, wailing
"Look out for me, look out."

The outgoing tide of sleep
Rolled you on your side,
Facing me on mine.
What then you did you'd said
You would: came on to me,
I mean full length of me.
Adjusting for the bones
You pressed me flat and
Contoured like a puddle,
A puddle all "sploopily,"
Undulating, smooth,
Which made a low and hungry
Sound, so sploopily
It poked us to adapt
Our figuration, find
Our universal joint,

The under-over-under
To get the inner-outer-
Inner.

Convergence

Rio Grande

North of Taos

The trail you want drops from the rim
Down steep switch-backs, to the deep of
That somber gorge, past a clear
Spring where damsel flies dandle
And mate over water their sky-blue wisps.
Your way leads on to a stretch of calm,
A pause between the rapids, where
No less intent on cleaving the world,
The Rio Grande runs quiet and sleek
And the sun midday strokes a glisten.
Here lies the capacious blue-black boulder
With room aplenty to sprawl full out,
To press its warm and obdurate chunk
To your cheekbone and ribs, your ringing ear,
Your overpopulated skull.
Let rock come up beneath you and hold you.

Too soon the dusk of a cliff will hide
The sun, will cool you, tell your body
Dark is coming, time to trek back.
From midnight shadow that overrides
You break into sun and ponderous heat,
And now you trudge from tree to tree,
Haul your bones from shade to shade.

Yet each twist of the trail amazes,
To view where you were, so far, so fast
It recedes, dwindles so quickly away.
The place, the spring, the azure damsels,
The cradling rock, have vanished from sight,
All blurred together, lost in shadow.

Convergence

In Taos High Country

Wild roses are blooming across the creek
And we pause to drink and breathe them in.
Farther up we admire a boulder
Patched with blue-green lichens: tokens.
Comes a spired stump like Shiprock,
Another steepled like Mont Saint Michel.
At last we rest in headwaters' basin
Resounding of cows climbed to the rim
Above us, tiny four-legged shapes
Figured against a cloud, as if
They mean to ascend to the mist beyond.

We two eat and talk of the past,
Years we ranged lonely, apart,
Before we found each other and joined
Our random ways. We couple our story
While our canyon's capillaries
Veer, converge and voice a creek,
Which meets another down from a lake,
And gathering others in their descent
Present a lively choir of waters
To rapids of Rio Grande (its source
A seep, a murmur far to the north),
Which after a long and roundabout

Wander and final thicket of towns
Surrenders itself and all its sounds
To the Gulf
       where creeks and rivers of praise
Dissolve in a sweeping level conclusion.

To the Peak

Ages the mountain is shedding,
Sharpening edges and cusps,
Chunking off boulders to tumble
Below in a heap of detritus
For ice to wedge and divide,
For swatches of lichen to mottle
In orange and turquoise green.

Amazed by desire we were;
Strong as an earth-breaking sprout
You lifted me out of myself.
It seemed we too were shedding,
Sloughing off cells and husks
Of the selves we thought we were.
No matter the piled years,
The years fell away, and we
Grew smooth and avid green.

From up on the crest of the peak
We could look down, beyond
Its halved and quartered talus
To the delicate lake in its lap,
To the place where we embraced—
One of the secret stars
That light up our map of time.

Savory Turbulence

Heat to seething
Four cups water,
Add one medium
Onion, chopped,
One tablespoon
Parsley, minced,
Two cloves, bay leaf,
Vinegar, oil,
Boil at roiling
Fifteen minutes;
Then slide in fish;
Serve with noodles,
Or with rice.

When I gaze into this seethe
Then I return in mind along
Tesuque Creek at melt of winter,
And I'm back to a certain place
Where stream is overwhelming stone,
Revolving bubbles and sticks and froth
Like a giant pan of broth.

Spring Runoff

Once again we went to find
Our special resource, our mother lode.
And so we climbed Tesuque Creek
In full and tumbling May,
Up among its rocky woods
And liquid rushing goods of snow.
Had to stop for breath, and speak
Some words that needed saying:

> I survived   I said   you too
> She said   you triumphed   we both
> We found each other   and
> More than made it   won our life

—words lost in parading water.

But thought played on: back
Aboard the GI going-home-train
Lifting me over Snoqualmie Pass
I knew well the adverse of
Delight but reveled even so,
Young in sex and crazy hope.

Relicts of confounding loss
We both in separate lives,
Lonely, far apart, would make

The common stumble into marriage
And come to similar lows.

Yet in each a trace of spring
Endured, a supple rivulet of
Love and lust, that when we met
Would press us close until we fused.

Come close, the water beckoned, join
In jubilation. And we partook.

The Santa Fe Special

Look for a flicker out the window
(No more sun, the sun's gone under),
Listen for a distant mutter,
Sniff in swelling breeze the musk,
The pheromone of rain and earth.
Now see horizons over-borne by
Blue-gray ink with midnight shading
Coming south our way for sure,
Not with spurious mist that peters
Out half-spent, but a true drench.
And now a hard particle
Raps the roof, and now another,
More until they crowd the land
With white and hopping dance, and we
Inhale the winter breath of hail
Relenting, melting, mixing dust,
Chamisa and piñon to conjure
Smell that tells us once again
Why we're here for keeps, and why
They dance and sing to beckon rain.
Holding hands we edge outside—
A blinding wink, a stunning crack—
We breathe again, and watch cascades
Of water make a sudden lake
That snakes its way up to our door.

The drop-rings widen, intersect
As roof receives and passes on
The slather to us, to our trees,
Our haggard land and maimed petunias.
After thunder wanders off
The patterns of splash prevail, and we
Regard each other and rejoice
And pueblos dance to thank the rain.
Implore
      pour
           roar
               adore.

Flood at Bandelier

The furious push that piled them up
Began in mountains stripped by fire
Followed by a flood of rain
That flumed the canyon, shoveled up
All the dead and rushed them down
To where each standing living tree
Would block them, hold them in a clutch
Of logs, limbs, shanks, scraps;
And caught in these entanglements
(Could not run to higher ground)
Ant, beetle, stinkbug standing
Upside down in final defiance,
Wasp the hunter poring over
Every nook of earth for spider,
Snake with its electric warning,
Its pattern undulating zigzag.

There we found a tiny toad,
Offspring of the aftermath,
Salmon-colored, hiding on
A darker stone. At a touch
It took a mighty leap away
And found in salmon pebbles safety.

Hope of Wildflowers

In a Time of Drought and Fire

Blue boon of blossoms held us,
Drew us like the bees that nuzzled
Down inside those small deep cups.
We were headed higher but
Compelled by the hue of them, a spell
That only deepest sky could conjure,
We turned aside to be with them.
And to follow bees in delving
In the depth of dark and luminous
Ultramarine, to nose around
And sing in a monotone of praise
Mmmmmm. Mmmmmm.

Unlike us—we won't be back—
The generations of gentians will
Come back and back, as will the children's
Children of the columbine
And scarlets of the paintbrush, and cool
Reds of the shooting stars that curl
And point their darts of flower downward
Toward the earth of their rebirth.

Celebration

on
Columbine Creek
July 4, 1994
South of Costilla
East of Questa

"Apple in bloom" I said.
"Lace," you said, a mantilla.
It spread a lavish commotion,
Welling up with hints
Of jade. Sunlight turned it
White and pearly; cloudy,
White and icy green.
Over a log it poured,
Ruled smooth and straight,
Then down, under and up
In a backward-curling wave
To break into rejoicing.
We were its only guests
That day. Two thousand miles
To cross the dreary nation
And find our celebration.
"This is what we came for,"
You said. But no more words,
Just listen and be merry.

Espiritu Santo

Espiritu Santo, the Spanish named it,
Holy Ghost, a canyon creek
Being born of sources high
In Pecos Wilderness, whose flanks
We clambered in traverse, climbing
From our prime of loving, stream-side.

      Take Spring for a start, by blues
Of iris, roses budding, aspen
New-fledged, shivering green: we walked
By almost silent sinewy water
Swelled by snow of upper zeniths,
Which overrode its boulders, breaking
Constant waves in racing onward.
The creek in all its power drew us
On from fork to narrowing fork
Toward its several beginnings,
Toward its intimate seeps and drips.

      An August cloudburst caught us out
And soused us, rain seemed to press
Our kiss, beating us together
As if to melt us into one.
The enormous hungry present

Overtook and lapped us up,
Inclining us to worship there.

      In October leaves were flying off
In migratory streams that flickered
Down to land another layer
Of fragrant shriveling where we walked.
Pale tall poles swayed, with now and then
A knock above, where one live tree
Upheld another, gray and dead.
The dwindling flow of Holy Ghost
Proceeded low and calm to Winter.
We knew when green came round again
Adoring shades would haunt that creek.

Chronicles of Conifer I

Upshot, upstart of soft offspring,
Six new inches of pinnacle,
Pale blue-green of spruce,
And paws slough off the mittens
That covered them through winter.
Time will stiffen and prickle;
Now they are pliant and tender,
We must take them in hand,
Greet these new growings.
Spire and purple buds
Rise further into peril,
Lightning will be searching.

Chronicles of Conifer II

Young-old
mast
past
bolt
volts
spire
fired

scorched
scarred
charred
gnawed
flayed
gray

bole
still
stands
green
spawn
enfolds
upholds

Chronicles of Conifer III

Tor
  tour
  torre
  yore
  tower

  wrack
  ramshackle
  barkback

  chart
  heartwood's
  hardcore
  umber ombre
  graven grey

  centenary
  tenement's
  beetle   riddles
  spider   tatters

hearts' haven's hulk
hands' cravings' carven core

Chronicles of Conifer IV

Hike cut short by rain
We poked along double cloaked,
Hoods drooped despondent,
Eyes to trail, sticks out
To ward off dripping herbage.
Then stopped, held by a
Deadfall, spilling riches.
Rain deepened color, carmine,
Burnt sienna, rust,
Down to cinnamon dust,
Disintegrating fir
In rain
               which gleamed on the greens
That slowly enclosed the reds,
But made them glow all the more.

Tenderly

All aspen up to crags,
The mountain breathes and shimmers,
Reminds him of a song
His dry lips try to whistle
But only sound a whisper,
A stark melody stripped
Of chords and words. And yet
It forms a cirrus of memory,
A GI-recruit-Kentucky-
Hot-August-evening cloud.
He toils on up the trail,
Stops for a drink of water,
Looks up at the high blue
Piercing between and because
Of yellows so bright they pull
Down the blue to interleaf.

"Self," his love calls him,
"Being" and "Bebe" she calls
His old self that plods
Stubborn to climb up high.
His knuckles and veins stick out
Like the roots and rocks ahead.
Self entails a youth
Whose torments melted away.

Remains a circle of faces,
Names and voices of soldiers
Never seen since then,
All old beings now.
Sounding a name is to strike
A chord, a face and voice
Spring alive and sharp,
Clear as they were in Korea,
Nineteen Fifty-Three.

He calls out to them:
Where are you? Still alive?
Did you see the world?
Marry and divorce?
Did you find true love?
        He tries to picture them
As old, but they won't let him.
"Forget that old man shit,
This is who we are."

Grove of Aspen

La Cueva Trail

No mob or crush, no jungle tangle,
Tall singles (some were twins),
This dignified crowd in a breeze
Slowly swaying, a knock, a creak,
A quiver high above, then still.
Mirroring one another they climbed
Receding toward a distant apex,
Catching sun, placing shadows
Each on each, titillating
Eyes to find the aisles through.

I turned and looked around for you
But I had wandered out of sight,
I couldn't find you. All at once
My moody heart foresaw the day
When one of us would not be there.

And then benign trees aligned
A slot, revealing down slope
Your sunlit hat and reading shape,
Part of the pattern of lights and darks.

Autumn Climb

Sunless sense of a luminous presence
High above, as I trudge up a trail
Much longer than I remember,
Gloomy and rank from a night of rain,
I climb in dark and heavy fatigue
But feel them airily there, each
Delicate lively leaf alert
To offer a tremor of light,
As one in dark of audience looks
Toward a radiance on stage,
Toward a music and dance of words.

October Angling

A climbing pine-roof checked the sun,
The splintered rays winked and turned
On every upstream step I took
Above the beavers' third landing.
To fix a bait, to plunk a hook
Would pull me near the bedside of
Our Lady of Drink, to hear her rush
And see her weaving over boulders sunk
And sunspots feeding on the floors
Of deep still rooms. To further dazzle,
Fresh-fallen aspen rounds were rocking
In her pools, to make a fretwork
Complicating any angling
For a shadow that might be dangling
In a hunger down below.
        For me the catch was her mosaic
            Flowing after, in my closing eyes.

Deciduous Lights

Now's
sideslip
wander
desultory
downward.
Yesterday's
day-before's
whiffs
withering
patterns
settle
micaceous
ground.
Latter's
former's
mix
black
years
before's.
Evergreens
net
straying
Christmas
hints.

Darkening
forest.
Scattered
lights.

Mesa Shadow, December

Two
roof
roamed
rimrock
    brim
    sharp
    limned
    escarp
    forehead
        aloof
        height
        leaped
        downswept
        foreshadowing

                night
                valley
                railway
                ville
                    roll
                    trolling
                    train-wail
                    horn-warning

                          raven
                          duo
                          roved
                            rode
                          wave
                          shade

Arid April

Guitar   thrummed
On open   strings

says

Board and bone
Honed by wind

Blown mouths   Faces of weeds
Of bottles booing   Begging at fences

Land and sun   Monotone of
Sky all dun   Known and un-

says

Deathless trash
Dust forever

Dust Devil

When piñons seethe along a furious
Path approaching helter skelter,
Beware trickery of air
That reaches down to enrage the dust,
Stampede the weeds and sticks,
Snatch up scraps and loose roofs
To bat around the sky.

Woman, Parched

The gloomy wandering cloud dropped
A dram and splashed a chip
That took the drink and lapped
It dry. A stuck-out lip
Of boulder caught another, though wet
Was not what rock was waiting for.

That was all. The storm would fret
And grope elsewhere to pour,
And dust could wait for drops.
The woman riding by could not.
She could swallow storms for sops,
Floods to slosh her hollows out.

Sky Theater

Some days it plays clouds,
Some, a blue main feature
Scored by moving dashes.
Today, tent for a preacher,

Screen of sky caught
Silent, cold fire
While earth in a black crowd
Huddled down before.

A flood of jeremiad
Orange fills my mind.
No title, credits, songs
Proclaim this soundless sign.

What gorgeous world disaster
Does the blaze insist,
What dream or memory?
We do repeat the past,

No good reminding us
Or warning of a smash.
Born to violence
Each wave will find its crash.

Hazardous Highway

A strange one-eyed speeder's
Coming up behind us,
Brighter than a headlight.
It's the moon in mirror,
The moon is on our tail.
Even with her pursuing,
Our high beams searching,
Lights exploding toward us,
My eye in sidelong glance
Sees stars piercing the night,
Streaming down behind
The black rim of the earth.
We're south of Taos, heading
Toward the canyon plunge,
No more road lamps, houses,
Just a duel of headlights,
A minor flicker under
The Major and Minor Bears,
Sirius and Orion,
Meteors darting, light-years,
Time out of mind.

Ray

Within a deep revealing casement
Out of the crazy rush of wind,
A window net of steady light
Imposes on the calcimine
A blazing calm, compelling eyes
To meet the stillness gazing in.

My house so honored by the ray
Turns away and travels on.
The wall creeps to white dusk;
Last light breaks across a table
Over crumbs, and warms my hands.

Its far source, the fire storm
Rages in a breeding vortex;
Twirl and distance make the blessing.
What could I not perceive or make
If I could pull that light inside?

But being earth and drawn to night
I wake in the dark, ignite a glimmer
Of imagined conversation,
Play a riff on a spectral keyboard,
Conjure up phantasmal creatures.
And so reject the knowing light.

Small Window

I

Four lights, four squares
Of outdoors pieced together,
Window quartered by a plus,
A cross prevailing through
Changing light and hue,
Provide an optic puzzle:
Which controls the eye,
Cross-bars or the view.

II

Imagine graying dawn
Become an aureate dazzle
Of medieval midnight sun,
A trecento crucifixion
Nailed against blank gold.
Gilt shoots back the light,
Figures wail and fall
Withered by blazing rays.

III

Blue dispels the sheen.
Blinding gold gives way
To a blue that drinks light,
Quattrocento afternoon
Recedes to a white horizon
Over Flemish roofs and valleys,
Tuscan stripes, arcades,
Friends greeting in a street.

IV

Painters saw greatly through
Small windows and praised
The scene behind crossbones.
Look beyond the branding iron,
Learn by heart the day-shine
Painters touched to hill,
Tower, jewel, eye,
Light that teaches us to see.

Is, Was, Will Be

Forest quotes sea, as sea
Unrolls a sound of leaves in waves.
They're all out now, quick to shiver.
Last year's blacken underfoot.
Farther up from here, the new-born,
Glossy from the darts of bud.
Higher up, gray winter still.
Two young hikers pass me, he
Bare to the waist, muscles gleaming,
She as supple as he and strong.
They stride ahead, soon out of sight.
As for myself, I keep hold
Of balance and my pair of sticks
To counter a certain downward bent.

Once out walking in the woods
We came across an aspen sapling
Stripped and skeletal and gray.
It stood alone amid a herd
Of ponderosa pines. In death
It had assumed its final figure,
Two long boughs curling down
And around in arcs that aimed to meet,
The others paired alike in arcs.
Their main stem undulated upward
In a supple-brittle stance.

Such counterpose of being, such
Delineation of itself
Stayed with us in mind and tendon,
Urged us to go back and find it:
Would that frailty still be there.
And there it was,
In final asana intact.
I took four angles and I drew
To keep the idea of it. Because
Time crashed on. We went again
And it was gone. Broken and dispersed.

When I'm gone, come on up here.
Find a sapling, pull it close.
Hear its silky sound, so lively
Even at rest a leaf will wave.
Before you let it go, immerse
Yourself within its green flutter.
Delicately it will tap
Your lips and nose, your arms and neck,
As if to find out what you are.

This book of poetry has been printed
on acid free paper.
The typeface is Adobe Jenson Pro.

Adobe Jenson is an old-style serif typeface drawn
for Adobe Systems by its chief type designer Robert
Slimbach. Its Roman styles are based on a text face cut
by Nicolas Jenson in Venice around 1470,
and its italics are based on those created by
Ludovico Vicentino degli Arrighi fifty years later.

www.ingramcontent.com/pod-product-compliance
Lightning Source LLC
Chambersburg PA
CBHW031143090426
42738CB00008B/1196